PONGE,
PASTURES,
PRAIRIES

PHILIPPE JACCOTTET
translated by John Taylor

BSE

ISBN: 978-0-9791495-8-0

BSE Books are distributed by
 Small Press Distribution
 1341 Seventh Street
 Berkeley, CA 94710
 orders@spdbooks.org
 www.spdbooks.org
 1-800-869-7553

BSE Books can also be
purchased at
 blacksquareeditions.org and
 hyperallergic.com

Contributions can be made to
 Off the Park Press, Inc.
 976 Kensington Ave.
 Plainfield, NJ 07060
 (Please make checks payable to
 Off the Park Press, Inc.)

To contact the Press write:
 Black Square Editions
 1200 Broadway, Suite 3C
 New York, NY 10001

An independent subsidiary of Off the Park Press, Inc.
Member of CLMP.

Publisher: John Yau
Editors: Ronna Lebo and Boni Joi
Design & composition: Shanna Compton

Cover art: *Arbres en hiver* (undated) by Anne-Marie Jaccottet. Watercolor and pencil. 18.6 × 20.6 cm. Courtesy of the artist.

I

Nîmes, 10 August 1988

VERY TALL, OLD, AND BEAUTIFUL TREES beyond high walls, as if one were going to enter the grounds of a park in Rome; a confusion which will be sustained by the sweltering heat, the bright sky, the chirping cicadas. A little exaltation and much sadness. FRANCISCUS PONTIUS, NEMAUSENSI POETA: this is indeed the right spot for his final dwelling place. Inside the walls, the great Protestant families have their graves, their mausoleums, almost all of which are also great in size, old, beneath these tall tees, this bright sonorous sky: "Big beautiful buildings of eternal structure // [. . .] Beautiful grounds and beautiful gardens, here in your cloister / you always have flowers and green shade . . ." This is definitely not the case here: the flagstones are falling apart, the monuments are becoming flaky, the vegetation is slowly growing wild again.

~

Are there more than twenty of us gathered in front of this vault with its door opened onto coldness and shadow? Scarcely. I cannot help but think of the state funeral, accompanied by Malraux's vehement funeral oration, held for Braque, one of his peers, and of that "Carousel of the Four Elements" which took place in "the most magnificent, the most deft, the most spirited manner" at the Louvre in 1606, as Francis Ponge noted with respect to Fautrier, not without a liking for pomp and glamor. Well, we are a long way from all that! But Ponge had also rather proudly declared, during an interview with Reverdy and Breton, "We have *chosen* poverty," "as low as possible," and perhaps this ceremony, which is almost not one, is thus more genuine, whereas the slightest citizen of Nîmes would have been surrounded by more people.

~

Ever a model of discretion, patience, and dignity, Odette long remained leaning against the Ponge family vault door, reopened that midsummer day, in plain daylight, onto the cold, onto what is worse than night. At the same time, I noticed that the ferns beneath the trees were ready to invade, sooner or later, what is called the "the final resting place," to triumph over the proudest, most massive funereal monuments. Suddenly, strangely, I saw her as an Electra on the threshold of a temple or at the door of a palace of tragedy, probably because Electra is a black-clad figure, apparently alone in her bereavement yet unvanquished, perhaps also because she turns up, for an instant, in Baudelaire, in a context of sorrow ("sending his heart and mind to a remote Electra who not long ago wiped his sweaty brow" . . .); moreover, to be truthful, upon this black-clad figure was briefly superimposed, as Ponge himself would have been the first to encourage us to see, another woman with almost the same name, Elvire, who is also noble, stern, pure, and black-clad, and who appears, unheeded, just before the final abyss opens. As if around Ponge's remains were hovering ungraspable spirits whom he had resolutely, obstinately, insisted upon keeping off his path, shadows that the sun of the loftiest and most radiant season would dispel once and for all, for our own great benefit. (It is truly to this end that the writer, and the master more than any other of his instrument, will have labored until the end.)

~

A pastor so extraordinarily modest and discreet that one initially took him, when he got off his bicycle and leaned it against the cemetery entrance wall, for a gardener's helper (and this, too, ultimately had something "rather good" to it, as Ponge liked to say, something more genuine in its near-absurdity), chose to read, at the edge of the vault, "because the deceased was a poet," he explained—he who had probably never read him—one of the psalms most familiar to anyone who has received a Christian education: "The Lord is my shepherd [. . .] He maketh me lie down in the green pastures . . ." I was still gazing at the ferns in the shade of the tall trees. Then Christian Rist gave a simple reading of "The Meadow": "Carried away suddenly by a sort of peaceful enthusiasm / In favor of a truth, today, which is green . . ." This kind of albeit distorted echo, over some thirty centuries, was thus perhaps even stranger and more striking than the rest (the vast, noble, abandoned cemetery and this burial, as if for an unknown person, of a writer so legitimately famous).

~

"This kind of instinct at once naïve, childlike, and wise"—these are the words pronounced by an eighty-year-old Ponge, in his rue Lhomond apartment, to Loïs Dahlin, as they were speaking about progress and the fact that, at least for language, there was "surely none. In ancient civilizations when it was clear that words and things were absolutely identical, one was in the field that Baudelaire called 'correspondences.' There was truly a correspondence between sensations and language. It is obvious that we are far from that. Most people have lost this sentiment, this kind of instinct at once naïve, childlike, and wise."

∼

When David, the future King David, wrote "The Lord is my shepherd," he had himself been a shepherd, by no means an idyllic shepherd (be it Góngora's), but a genuine shepherd with a shepherd's hands, and he had hiked up and down those "green pastures"; all of that—the herds, the scarce grass and water—made up his world; and it must have been hardly less real, back then, to see another world showing through it: eternal grass, eternal water, and, at their edges, an invisible yet powerful shepherd on whom one could rely as if on a father or a prince. A world as harsh, in some respects much harsher, than ours, thirty centuries older, but a world that can be imagined as being still relatively simple and solid, coherent, so that poems, back then, could naturally express trust and, by expressing it, fortify it.

~

Today, thirty centuries later, some human beings still say these words, finding comfort in them, cherishing clear or confused hopes on them; such people are relatively few in number, even as genuine shepherds have become few in number, if not herds and pastures. Shepherds seem to be among the last survivors of a very ancient world (the one in which perhaps reigned an instinct "at once naïve, childlike, and wise") and, as such, we glorify them with our nostalgia. For a poet as civilized as Rilke, an "end of the lineage" kind of poet if one will, and, in many respects, very remote from Ponge (who is nevertheless also surely a great poet), the shepherd glimpsed in Spain, standing "on the earthy mountain ridge," is still a literary figure capable of accommodating, by means of his close link with the original world, a god—but an unknown one; he is a model for the modern poet, gone astray, almost spectral, who lacks "the mitigation of the herd." ("In turn he lingers and moves off, like the day. / And shadows of clouds / go through him as if space / were thinking thoughts for him, slowly.")

~

I have not distanced myself all that much from Ponge by taking these paths onto which I was led by the two texts read "on the brink of the abyss," in Nîmes, on 10 August 1988. I know well that the "green truth" that Ponge sought to conjure up on the page was not encumbered with what is invisible, since it had enough to do with what is visible, and that it had rather, instead, risen up, sometimes in anger, against the invisible: Malherbe's laurel ("His doors open, Apollo lets / The lovely evergreen leaves / Keeping names from aging / Be gathered as one wishes"—how Ponge liked to recite these lines of verse, with what luminous enthusiasm he articulated them, to the extent of almost convincing me, indeed, and how I like to recall him in those moments!): thus Malherbe's laurel or the terrestrial meadow near Chambon, and not Rilke's laurel that is "a little darker than any / other green, with tiny waves at each leaf's edge (like the wind's smile)" . . .

However, Francis Ponge's way of waging battle throughout his lifetime, of gathering himself into a ram (in both the animal and military senses of the word) and of charging, sometimes at the expense of his best friends (of course, on the level of ideas and tastes), of goading his adversary, of trumpeting out his challenges, including his not necessarily convincing slogans; his way also of using everything in his arsenal and thus running the risk of tiring or exasperating his reader; his extreme arrogance (perhaps a weapon against deep doubts); his excessive intolerance (compatible with the most generous enthusiasms); his detours, needless repetitions, also his complications bordering on mannerism . . . Wasn't all this—this beautiful battle (which was always, in any event, courageous, manly, out in the open)—the fault of those thirty centuries, each one of which seems to have distanced us a little further from "this kind of instinct at once naïve, childlike, and wise," and an attempt to find in a different way, somehow and almost by force, the "true" grass, the "true" original vegetation? Because it was not possible to make do with less?

~

As to "truth," however, it seems to me that Ponge had become, with time, less self-confident; among other things, I am thinking of these lines from January 1964, after Braque's death and in regard to him:

The mind moves at who knows what speed, Truth much more slowly.
I must even say that, as far as I am concerned, SHE takes more and more time to catch up with me.
In a general way, She does not seem to be something to attain, but to await.
All that we can do, instead of dashing off to pursue her, is to slow down our mind so that She can join us.
The notes that we compile, the words that we align, are for this purpose only.
When one day She comes up to our level (as one says), and touches us on the shoulder, this is a surprise which, in turn, nails us to the ground; we recognize Her because of her extraordinary face.

(That Ponge, who boasts less than all the other ones, is the greatest one.)

~

One imagines that, in his old age, he had, all the same, somewhat put aside the hope driving him when I knew him in his rue Lhomond apartment just after the end of the war (of which he in fact spoke little, but all the more so, for hours on end, of his work): the hope of changing the world by changing poetry. The beautiful utopia ("The year will have no more winter, the day no more shadow, / and countless pearls / will blossom among the gravel in the Seine") had, in all likelihood, distanced itself even further. Beyond his window, the splendid sun of reason had become reenveloped in wisps of haze, some of them, in fact, more than suspect; others, perhaps (those of Elsinore?), which he had a little too proudly, out of defiance, disregarded. This very old question, not only for me but for all human thought, emerged once again in my mind, moved and saddened between those two written "grass pastures" that came into contrast on the brink of a cold abyss where, to be sure, the warmhearted friend and great craftsman of language was no longer there except in his most vain and deceiving effigy.

~

"The muses, the nine beautiful fairies" . . . : may they better than angels, if this were his wish, keep him alive, whole, and nearby like another summer sun.

There are festivities and festivities

HERE, I HAD INITIALLY PLANNED TO ADD a few pages reiterating my arguments, in praise of Ponge, which I had already put forward, in different forms, in one or another of the many articles that I will have devoted to this writer between 1946 and 1986. After thinking it over, it did not seem necessary to preserve those pages, which were unnecessarily repetitive. I had drafted them especially out of qualms, fearing that one would forget, when reading what follows, the admiration and affection that had remained intact in me with respect to Ponge. And, after all, for a reader tempted to look up those praises, I would only have to direct him to them, from which I find nothing to remove today.

Simply, beginning with my entirely instinctive reaction to the dual reading, in Nîmes, in front of the mortal remains of the poet, I have felt the need to specify, at first for my own use, what separated me (and had always more or less explicitly separated me) from this oeuvre. And there was no reason for me to fear that I would be reproved for having waited until his death to express this distance because I had clearly asserted it in 1965, when *Pour un Malherbe* appeared, and again in 1967: because I could evidently not subscribe to the hierarchy that Ponge had proclaimed in his book at the time, even *cum grano salis*, by situating his hero, Malherbe, above Góngora and especially Cervantes and Shakespeare.

Back then, concerned above all to pay tribute to the striking, salubrious singularity of Ponge, I did not develop the reservations evoked only at the end of my study of *Pour un Malherbe* and in the "Note" that fills it out in *L'Entretien des Muses*. In the following pages, instead of developing those reservations, I will do nothing more than take a few steps in that different direction towards which, after all, I have never stopped venturing—by groping, it seems to me today, ever less often.

∼

Facing Ponge's mastery, notably in some of his most perfectly accomplished short texts—of which *Le Parti pris des choses* (Partisan of Things) puts forth the first and perhaps best examples—, it can happen that one is almost tempted to applaud, as if they were the marvel-inspiring feats of a juggler; and it takes a lot to carry this off, as in a pure, lighthearted circus act with no ulterior motive. But I also know that I run the risk of sometimes feeling too enclosed under this big top, of lacking air; delighted by the feat, indeed, but not absolutely fulfilled. I would prefer more space and more uncertainty; as if the trick were almost too successful to be completely "true."

∼

Nonetheless, it must be added—and I had paid tribute to this aspect too, as was appropriate, for *Le Soleil placé en abîme* (The Sun Placed in the Abyss)—that Ponge soon increased the boundaries of his art and ventured much farther. Basically, he wasn't all that close to Chardin or to Braque, however admirably he praised both (and this propensity to praise, this warmth in his approbation, are virtues which will always nourish my affection for him). By nature, his art is much less well-behaved, its tone less intimate and less muffled, its movement less restrained. With his explosive, pugnacious, swaggering personality, he soon trespassed limits, for our great pleasure, that one part of himself—the most reasonable, severe, also theoretical part—had assigned to him, to produce at least the elements, the rough drafts, the projects of a festivity in a noble, proud and spirited style, such as the festivity he will evoke one day in regard to Fautrier, and such as *The Sun Placed in the Abyss* will magnificently deploy its pomp.

All the same: even more widely open, and closer to a royal triumph, than juggling, this kind of festivity was carried off to the sound of cheers. Whereas the reading of Hölderlin (and if his name now comes to mind, it is because of those festivities of which he also had dreamt more than a century beforehand) induces no eagerness to applaud; as if there were festivities and festivities . . .

Two of Ponge's Heroes, or Harbingers

AND THE FIRST ONE: Malherbe, the great model to whom Ponge devoted a more-than-three-hundred-page speech for the defense, which he elaborated between 1951 and 1957 and in which he imagines Malherbe sitting at the same table as Góngora, Cervantes, and Shakespeare, after which—listen well: "Only Góngora, when the dessert is on the table, can keep pace with him (but the former slows down imperceptibly), whereas Cervantes and Shakespeare have already, for some time, clearly stopped making sense of what is going on)." As far as provocation goes, we have more than our share! But weren't these outrageous excesses, behind which I seem to glimpse the author's somewhat Chinese smile, in one aspect, because I have spoken of battles, the right shot of strong alcohol that he needed to leap to the attack of the old lyrical citadels and to demolish the ancient, never-ending "merry-go-round"—to use his term.

~

It is not less certain that Malherbe's poetry is also able to provoke in the reader, in places, an initially surprising jubilation. I have already recalled the lines that Ponge so enthusiastically cited; but here is the entire strophe:

Apollon à portes ouvertes
Laisse indifferemment cueillir
Les belles feuilles tousjours vertes
Qui gardent les noms de vieillir ;
Mais l'art d'en faire des couronnes
N'est pas sceu de toutes personnes,
Et trois ou quatre seulement,
Au nombre desquels on me range,
Peuvent donner une louange
Qui demeure eternellement.

[His doors open, Apollo lets
The lovely evergreen leaves
Keeping names from aging

Be gathered as one wishes;
But the art of making crowns of them
Is not known to everyone,
And only three or four,
Including me,
Can give a praise
That lasts eternally.]

Without question, the tension of a lyre reduced to
the minimum number of strings, the rigorous diction,
and the perfect concert of terms founded on the basso
continuo of a proud and manly moral doctrine can
produce this jubilation. All the same: in such lines, the
richness and variety of the natural world (a shortcom-
ing of which neither Ponge's nor even Góngora's oeuvre
can be accused) will always be lacking for me; many
dimensions of the human world (which confirms that
Cervantes and Shakespeare have an obvious preemi-
nence, whatever Ponge thinks) will always be lacking
for me; and still lacking for me will be something else
(and now Dante whom, unless I am mistaken, Ponge
never mentioned, must indeed be evoked), something
towards which, as I have now understood, these pages
are heading without my having initially intended them

to do so: "the extraordinary face" of Truth (it's Ponge, as we have seen, who capitalizes the word); "she," as he also writes, who is less to attain than to await; she who might have fled because of his excessive containment but who will perhaps have, in fact, "caught up with" him sometimes without his knowing so, in his forgetful or distracted moments?

∼

On the other hand: isn't there in this glorification of the art of glorifying, if not the beginning (it goes back much earlier), at least one of the first striking manifestations of that narcissistic turning back of the poet towards himself as a poet, towards his work, towards the tools of his trade, of that obsession with language which reigns today in literature? If one must adore gods, then one might as well choose other, more remote, more un-graspable ones.

∼

When *Les Indes galantes* was triumphantly restaged at the Opera of Paris in 1952—at the heart of those years which, for him, were those of his greatest vigor—Francis Ponge paid a tribute to Rameau that was no less impassioned (in "La Société du génie"). He proclaims Rameau to be "the artist who interests me the most deeply in the world"; his musical oeuvre is "the pure diamond of our intellectual crown—because it joins, on that nocturnal forehead, the jewels of abolished civilizations"; his style "is of the kind that awakens: male, energetic, and ardent." Doubtless . . . However, with respect to Rameau as to Malherbe, isn't Ponge getting heated up a little while he is speaking (it seems to me that in German this can be expressed in a stronger, more compact way: *sich heißreden*), to put more conviction into his argument because these two are among his standard-bearers? For me, in any event, I am unable to prefer Rameau to Schubert, to Beethoven, even less so to Mozart; and going back earlier, to Monteverdi or to Bach. Is this the sign that my culture is not entirely French? The remains of an incorrigible Romanticism? What's to be done? This is how I am. And if one wishes to restrict oneself to an art of measure, number, and rigor, can there be any doubt that Bach outmatches Rameau, by rather far?

(I well know that announcing preferences in this way is simplistic. I resign myself to doing so to move ahead more quickly and to help me to understand better, step by step, what separates me from an author with whom such a long interaction has linked me.)

~

And indeed with respect to Bach: while recently listening to the *Goldberg Variations*, I became aware of the extent to which it was difficult for me to find analogies on an intuitive level to translate, even approximately, the sovereign beauty; whereas I had sometimes managed to do so, somehow, with Purcell or Schubert. I noted down only this: a sentiment of plenitude, explainable by the fact that one seemingly feels "inside" the music, with no place remaining for any tension, a "Sehnsucht" towards something else in the distance, something hidden from sight; an equilibrium, evidently, an order, but of the highest kind, and without tyranny. It is certain that one is not tempted to speak of "the heart," of feelings, of passion; even less so, to evoke landscapes (or, if need be, constellations, but such as would be visible in plain daylight, by no means against a dark background); nor, furthermore, faces or bodies; not even angels or gods.

Perhaps, as I also noted down, is it as if reason were jubilating? (However, at the time, I had not yet reread Ponge evoking Rameau.) Even adding, just after I had finished listening: "there is something, at times, that is martial, conquering, a force delighted to blossom, a jubilatory mathematics." And this, too: "The rapid movements do not more specifically suggest dances, nor anything whatsoever that is *heated*. Instead, an explosion of limpid figures, a free playing with time, almost always a deftness (yet let me insist: no elves or angels), a kind of winged reason? Or as if all sorts of impulsions, momentums at intentionally conquering speeds, find themselves settled, like a completely decanted wine, without ceasing to be lively."

Up to now, nothing very distant from Ponge's praise of Rameau. I almost seemingly join him here or there. But then there are the slow variations; they force me to seek my references much farther, at the very limit of what is graspable; and to compare them, always immediately after I have listened to the music, "to what one could hear, having crossed the Lethe in Dante's *Purgatory*, words and inflexions at the highest level of the universe . . ." Nearing in this way, once again, that which goes beyond the limits within which Ponge always ferociously kept himself, or wanted to keep himself, whereas he had himself nonetheless been able to transgress them, without wishing to do so, or at least pushed them farther outwards.

Always Limits

THE TEXT FROM WHICH I MOST BENEFITED from Ponge's method, which he formulated for the first time in *Le Carnet du bois de pins* (The Pine Woods Notebook)— the integration into the published book of the successive approaches made to endow the mute object with speech—is "Working at a Place known as L'Étang" in *Landscapes with Absent Figures*. It is certain that I would not have written that text, and a few others of the same ink, if I had not read Ponge; for I am not really, and this is the least that one can say, a pioneer.

Rereading those pages today, I tell myself that Ponge did not lack forbearance in regard to me, because the warmth of his friendship by no means lessened after the publication of the book. Yet a text like that had everything needed to irritate him; at least, to irritate the doctrinaire in him, who was perhaps therefore less present than I thought . . . Let's try to be absolutely simple here. I would not have the nerve to oppose my trial-and-error experiments to Ponge's ever-vigorous, exact, and tonic prose. This is not the issue. What is at stake is a movement of the mind, an orientation of one's way of looking. And I cannot help but notice that I am using here, indeed without thinking too much about it, Ponge's method of going in the opposite direction from the one in which he was walking with such a confident stride.

First of all, the starting point is different. In principle, Ponge can, and wants to, speak of anything: a pebble, a wooden crate, a boiler for washing laundry, a potato—things which can be elaborated and from which a small (or big) verbal machine can be set to work (but with what in sight? I will return to this). As to lyric poetry, it is born from an unexpected encounter, by no means motivated, but in tune with the poet's intimate nature, to the extent of immediately creating a specific emotion in him; in fact, one clearly sees that there are (if I may greatly simplify) poets of spring and others of summer, poets of water and others of fire, poets of dawn and others of night. The starting point of a text like my "Working at the Place known as L'Étang" is the "fleeting impression" which I have seemingly discovered at such a point in the space and time of my life, which I feel compelled to "decipher," and, even more strangely, which I suppose to be "veridical" (a supposition which, so one can fear, is solely founded upon the depth and intensity of the emotion that it brings). Of course, there is, as with Ponge, a "lesson" to draw from the world; but each lesson is greatly remote from the next one. It is here that the difference in function, in orientation, is revealed.

Everything—I think I can say this—everything that has given rise in me to a poem or a poetic prose piece has done so, it seems to me, because an opening has taken place in the wall of appearances; an opening through which, in addition, a happy light did not necessarily pass; what rushed through might have been frightful. "Everything is promise," says a passage of "Working at the Place Known as L'Étang"; and another passage: "only the inaccessible blooms" . . . "I see the shadow of the unlimited shining in the distance" is the last sentence of the text, the least unfaithful translation, even if still vague, of the "supposedly veridical inscription." The goal or, rather, the result being therefore to open, to let through; to push back the limit or, at least, to air, always, out of a horror of suffocation which might well ultimately come (the memories, among the oldest ones that I have, suggest this to me) from childhood terrors. Ponge's writings aim at opposite ends. He would plug up these kinds of interstices, to finish once and for all with what they seem to let pass; not, of course, out of fear; but out of a refusal to fear what he judges to be out of reach, if not to say spectral, out of a refusal to waste his time, his energy, his radiance, his fire, amidst those wisps of haze.

I admire and still like today the brilliance of this choice, of what it enabled Ponge to create in language. However, I find something too restrictive in this (with respect to my tastes, or better: to my experience). Let's say that the admiration in which I have held him will not have been able to keep me from roaming, more in accordance with my nature; perhaps to lapse as well into some very ancient errors because they seemed necessary to me if one wishes to give an account of Being in its entirety, and because there would be a chance, after all, that they would lead me further.

The "pure springing forth"

THESE REFLECTIONS WERE BORN in front of the vault in Nîmes where, in the scorching August heat, Ponge's mortal remains had been placed. It is not surprising that my thoughts have ended up joining those noted down in 1968, as the conclusion of *L'Entretien des Muses*, after having undergone a deep ordeal: the death of a man who had been almost as close to me as a father. After getting over the shock, I then wrote about my impression that in our literature had been formed closed systems inside of which only a clan language was spoken, a clan language that was often overburdened with references and that could only remain impenetrable to anyone living outside those systems—that is, to nearly everyone. I was notably thinking at the time, without saying so, of those passages in Ponge's oeuvre that seem to have been written, let's say, "for Paulhan";

as of—and in this case I mentioned Michel Deguy, who is, nevertheless, a first-class poet—the invasion of writing by a certain philosophical language. I was thinking of the perilous way in which poetry turns back on itself. In this respect, my attitude has not changed. Everything happened as if a sorting out had taken place in my mind between what stands up and what doesn't, between what remained fitting, or not, at the bedside of one who is dying and about which I was unafraid to speak in *Leçons*; as during that other summer, in front of the open grave. My reaction was probably a little simple, indeed simplistic; I didn't even promise myself to be rigorously faithful to it; it was nonetheless mine and, whatever its legitimacy, useful.

For what stood up, what stands up, to some extent, to death (not death that is imagined or thought of, but the presence of a dead person who was close to you—without even speaking of pain, which is another matter), could be not only, nor necessarily, the Word (in the religious sense and for whatever religion); not only what one has the right to call, while weighing one's words, the sublime (of which I see in this precise moment the most appropriate image in Dante, in Dante's proud, painful footsteps as he goes from the lowest to the highest place in the mountain of the world; not necessarily "the perfectly accomplished" (which runs the risk of shattering against such an obstacle). No, it could be something else again, apropos of which has come to mind the double adjective forged by Hölderlin in "The Rhine": *reinentsprungenes*, the "pure springing forth," what surges out pure," which, as he informs us, is an "enigma."

Moreover, I believe that Hölderlin's "pure springing forth" is not very far from Rimbaud's "spark of gold of Nature as light," in whom the search for this is essential; this would legitimate the "myth" created around his oeuvre by giving him a wholly separate place in modern poetry. That Rimbaud was indeed closer to the source than any of his contemporaries can be heard immediately, I believe, so there is no need to say more; even if the impossibility to found this difference by using reason can disturb, can make the text, and the shock it produces, suspicious to a too positivist mind.

~

Would it henceforth be too simple, or insubstantial, to imagine that "what springs forth pure" could purify the worst horrors by calcination, or cleanse them through baptism? In books, this springing forth seemingly happens only instantaneously, in a sentence, in a line of verse, which we are subsequently tempted, for want of anything better, to qualify as "magical" because of its intense effect on us; in music, it might be a theme, a few measures, a simple modulation (such as with the eloquent examples in Schubert); here, as there, hardly more than an inflection. (And I have sometimes, not thought, which is easy, but felt that poetry and music, in their movements of magic, of grace, precisely seem to shift the movement of the world, to sway the rigor of destiny.)

∼

Yet what is the "pure"? Would it be a pure moral order, a disincarnated angelism? No, it wouldn't. Instead, it would be a freshness illustrated most convincingly by the dawn and the water of torrents, but which could also spring out at any moment of the day, of a lifetime, of history, through surprising, admirable projections—which are pure of what? Of all violent, irrepressible lies and artifices, as if one found oneself suddenly, once again, yet without having planned it, without understanding how, even if one is perhaps in the evening of one's life and in the evening of the world, very close to the source, which is the enigma that one can solve only by means of an enigma.

∼

And, coming back to literature: does this intuition explain why I subscribe more willingly, and without any reservations, to what Ponge called his "quick sketches" ("pochades") than to several of his more elaborated texts? Does this mean that I must be put among the supporters of the "natural style" which was defended by Pascal and to which our author opposes a "concert style" of which Malherbe is, in his eyes, the hero? In fact, I think that Ponge, in this case, was aiming at the wrong target: what Pascal means by a "natural style" would be better defined as an "invisible style"; to his mind, the great writer is someone of whom one doesn't even notice that he writes well. In this, Pascal is opposed less to Malherbe than to all the "precious" writers, to the virtuosos, of which our time is infested.

This preference, to which responds, in painting, a pronounced taste for the sketch rather than for the accomplished painting (for example, evidently, in the work of Rubens or, closer to us, of Constable), probably stems from the fact that in a time of such vast, serious disorder, *order* in art needed to be extraordinarily strong, persuasive, that is, founded, so as not to seem stilted or artificial to us. It is thus unsurprising, within our ruins, that the fragment and the first draft generally seem more "genuine," more "fitting," than any ensemble albeit conceived in imitation of the most noble models or in accordance with an intuition of a forthcoming *order* of which would it would be, as it were, the precursor, as, I think, Ponge, with all his energy wished, intended, hoped would be the case and in part carried out in a great book like *Le Soleil placé en abîme* (The Sun Placed in the Abyss); or also, in a less ample but more accomplished way, in the *Sapates* illustrated, in the most beautiful sense of the word, by Braque's engravings.

∼

At the beginning of *My Creative Method*, one can read this, dated 18 December 1947: "I do not feel whatsoever assured of the assertions that I happen to make during a discussion. Those opposed to mine seem almost always as valid; let's say, to be more exact: neither more nor less valid. They convince me, they easily demolish me, if not with respect to some truth, at least the fragility of my own opinion. Likewise, the value of the ideas most often appears in an inverted ratio to the ardor employed to utter them. The tone of firm belief (and even of sincerity) is adopted, it seems to me, as much to convince oneself as for convincing the interlocutor, and perhaps even more to *replace* the firm belief." My first reaction, when I reread this, was to consider that Ponge, this time, was coming on too strong, if one kept in mind some of the assertions made in *Pour un Malherbe*, for example, and many others; and in such and such a conversation, in which one put forward assertions in opposition to his, one did not really have the impression at all that, to his mind, they seemed as valid as his . . . Now that I have given this matter some thought, his claims are perhaps not so paradoxical after all. And my note in *L'Entretien des Muses* remains pertinent, I think: "The sentiment that I had when reading *Pour un Malherbe*, despite all that it provides [. . .], namely that in the three places where the author speaks of *things* (the temples of Nîmes [. . .], the petroleum fire in Rouen and 'the joy of this bouquet of beans' [. . .]), his book attained its maximum density and brilliance, is not a sentiment to ignore. I find it again, after thinking about this, with respect to all his oeuvre. His work gets warm (and warms me) only in passages where words rub up against things."

In passing, a small question, apropos of metaphor: doesn't one who makes use of metaphor other than by playing or in a completely disinterested way, necessarily cross a boundary? Isn't it perhaps as if a "fitting" metaphor presupposed, or produced, surging forth from the relation that it asserts, that it invents (in one or the other senses of this verb), a superior light with which it crowns itself, and beyond which one would not be able to explain the power that it holds over us?

Two Examples

*En se rejoignant
elles deviennent silencieuses
les eaux de montagne*

[When they flow together
the mountain waters
become silent]

WHAT DID BUSON MEAN when he wrote this haiku, if not, apparently, that when mountain torrents rush down into the valley, the noise of their waters can no longer be heard? What a discovery!

However, it happens that the extreme concision of the haiku, by letting only four elements pass into the words—the mountain, the waters, their confluence, and the ensuing silence—and by associating them, as the poem does, into a movement and a kind of meta-morphosis, enables the poet to give rise, amid what is almost nothing, to an open space in which the encounter of these elements—each one of which is linked for us to a great number of inner correspondences, memories, and dreams—can take on its widest and deepest resonance. And this occurs, furthermore, without the poet's giving the impression of touching upon this resonance, and without what he has jotted down—which, formulated differently, would be at the limits of insignificance—being in any way put in the forefront. (Here, Truth with Ponge's capital "T," which one must less attain than await, is not even awaited, but seemingly forgotten . . .)

~

Someone who is merely walking down a path, who has an unburdened mind, who has a goal or not, and perhaps it is better if he has none, just anyone, perhaps guided, in any case accompanied for a long time by the noise of the torrents and waterfalls, a youthful noise spurring his walk, discovers, further on, further down, once he has reached the plain with its thicker grasses, its taller, leafier trees, discovers that the waters, however more abundant, flow more quietly and do not disturb the silence. Perhaps he too, one day, as his life progresses, will feel calmer, slow down his pace, make fewer movements with his hands, cut back on his use of words, and all this indeed because he will have become richer and stronger. And it could be said that, not much later (Buson will be sixty-four years old that year, with not much time left to live), but at thousands of kilometers from there, another wanderer, much less anonymous, less effaced, echoes him in his own way when he writes in pencil on the wooden paneling of a hunting lodge above Ilmenau, on 6 September 1780, the few words—a little more than a few words, all the same—of the poem that begins thus:

Über allen Gipfeln
Ist Ruh' . . .

[Over all the heights
is quiet . . .]

It will remain, throughout our own day and age, one of his most famous poems.

~

By comparing these two short poems by wanderers, haven't I joined back up with the "enigma of what is pure" that I have questioned for such a long time? And shouldn't I realize—if I gathered, even if only mentally, the numerous fragments of poetry, from all times and places, which I have cited as examples of the highest specific power of this art—that most of them converge towards this point? Aren't I going to be induced to say, once again, that the ten words of the French translation of Buson (and, surely, even more so, the traditional seventeen syllables of the original, which I don't know) are limpid enough to ring, at the bedside of a dying person, like a temple bell announcing that a door is going to open? Or that the twenty-four words of Goethe's poem envelop the heart so well that, under this coat, it could get across the last mountain pass without succumbing to the cold?

Pastures and Prairies

"THE LORD MAKETH ME lie down in green pastures" . . .
Words that come to us from the depths of the desert,
where mirages are born; words torn from a dry tongue
or a dry soul; words that have come back from the
depths of time. Back then, things were simpler: one had
a body, which had to be fed, refreshed, whose thirst had
to be quenched; one had herds, with the same needs.
And one also had a soul and, for this soul, an invisible
shepherd and invisible pastures, but no more dubious
than the other pastures. One had two kinds of thirst,
and two kinds of water. Seeing one kind surging forth
energetically or flowing quietly meant receiving the
reminder or the promise of the other one. There were
precise rules and a solid hope. There was a great sim-
plicity and a great force, both of which were integral
parts of words, as each also was present in sculptures

and monuments. There is no doubt about this when one sees them, in museums, and even more convincingly if they have remained in their original location, bound by iron to the place where they stand. Yet all this involved idols or homes for idols. It is as if it took the greatest force and the greatest possible simplicity to master, to cajole, to retain the too-close gods. To be able to rise to the occasion when facing what nothing could protect one from: storms, death. Today, perhaps death has remained as immense, as ungraspable as back then, but that no monument, no word, can pit itself against it anymore. Perhaps death is, today, the last thing that looks like the gods of ancient times.

~

Here, I wish to open a digression, as one opens a door onto a garden. When I was seeking, also last year, to hail the blossoming quince tree, to understand the flowering, to display that green and white blazon, I thought of the *Vita Nova*; but also, more remotely, of the pastoral play *The Winter's Tale*, where the magic of the theater is exerted in a more ingratiating way through the supremely gracious fusion of metaphors and metamorphoses: it is another *Triumph of Flora*, and one of the most beautiful examples.

The two lovers in the middle of the feast are disguised: the prince as a shepherd, the shepherdess as a queen; and the shepherdess, Perdita, doesn't know that she is in fact a queen. And here she is offering flowers, lavishing them; these flowers are not "mere" flowers (or, rather, they are flowers in their plenitude, with their pollen of the invisible); they are linked to the seasons, to those of nature as to those of our lives; they are linked to the gods: to Proserpina abducted by Pluto, to Juno, to Cytherea, to Phoebus (that is, to the greatest dimensions of the universe); and birds such as swallows and wood pigeons, no less laden with meaning, fly in the vicinity.

What is celebrated here, what is at the heart of the feast, is spring, resurrection; it is around this time of the year and of life, and around this hope, that revolve the singing, the dancing, the very poem; and it is this that the poem dons, with its precious cloth of metaphors; it is also Perdita herself who celebrates spring, with her grace lost and, soon, recovered through the power of love.

Perdita: . . . Oh, these I lack
To make you garlands of, and my sweet friend,
To strew him o'er and o'er!

Florizel: What, like a corpse?

Perdita: No, like a bank for love to lie and play on.
Not like a corpse; or, if not, not to be buried,
But quick and in mine arms. Come, take your
     flowers.
Methinks I play as I have seen them do
In Whitsun pastorals. Sure this robe of mine
Does change my disposition.

Will the thought of death, here surging forth unexpectedly, and playfully, ever have been more tenderly, more amorously enveloped in words, more efficaciously metamorphosed within the incense of poetry? "No, like a bank for love to lie and play on": as if there were nothing more sovereign to set in opposition to death than a grassy bank and tender arms. Perdita is similar to Flora; she is a body enveloped only in flowers to disperse death; vegetation and milk.

I cannot close the door of this enchanted place, because I have it in my heart. It is henceforth a part of me, such that, if I come back to those grassy embankments deserted by festivities and even by shadows of festivities, they will never, even in a different form, be completely deserted.

~

Orchards and prairies. Perhaps nothing affects me more strongly, more inevitably, than those places in nature. Orchards and prairies keep me ensnared like a prisoner in love with his prison. However, to restrict myself to pastures, meadows, and prairies, I see clearly that it is not in the language of the Bible that grass speaks to me; language does not appeal, perhaps can no longer appeal to symbols. Nor is it in Ponge's language anymore (at least in the language that he proclaims, that he displays, if not in the one that sometimes escapes him). It is a language more difficult to grasp, to translate. Its sound will have surprised me more than once as being more mute than insistent. And, in a certain way, so full of goodness that it will have seemed to respond to my revolt when facing hell, the stormy hell into which every one of us runs the risk of being hurled one day. Saying this can seem unacceptable; as grandiloquent as absurd, futile, improper. "Ein Rätsel ist reinentsprungenes"—I find once again Hölderlin's words quoted above. They could be transposed: everything that springs out pure is an enigma, if not even: the limpidity of the source is an enigma; the limpidity of the grass, of flowers in the grass, of prairies, is forever undecipherable. Somewhere I have read these words by Angelus Silesius: "God is the green of the meadows." It seems to me that these words can be joined to the other, later ones, and fortify them.

~

Going forward, or be it even wandering in this sense, was no longer whatsoever Dante's prodigious ascension to Paradise, "faster than lightning returning home"; it was no longer Saint Augustine's superb Latin in *The Confessions*:

> Corpus pondere suo nititur ad locum suum. Pondus non ad ima tantum est, sed ad locum suum. Ignis sursum tendit, deorsum lapis. Ponderibus suis aguntur, loca sua petunt. Oleum infra aquam fusum super aquam attollitur, aqua supra oleum fusa infra oleum demergitur; ponderibus suis aguntur, loca sua petunt.

Minus ordinata inquieta sunt ; ordinantur et quiescunt. Pondus meum amor meus; eo feror, quocumque feror. Dono tuo accendimur et sursum ferimur; inardescimus et imus. Ascendimus ascensiones in corde et cantamus canticum graduum. Igne tuo, igne tuo bono inardescimus et imus, quoniam sursum imus ad pacem Hierusalem . . .

["A body inclines by its own weight gravitates towards the place that is fitting for it. Weight does not always tend towards the lowest place, but one which suits it best, for though a stone falls, flame rises. Each thing acts according to its weight, finding its right level. If oil is poured into water, it rises to the surface, but if water is poured on to oil, it sinks below the oil. This happens because each acts according to its weight, finding its right level. When things are displaced, they are always on the move until they come to rest where they are meant to be. In my case, love is the weight by which I act. To whatever place I go, I am drawn to it by love. By your Gift, the Holy Ghost, we are set aflame and borne aloft, and the fire within us carries us upward. Our hearts are set on an upward journey, as we sing the song of ascents. It is your fire, your good fire, that sets us aflame and carries up upward. For our journey leads us upward to the peace of the heavenly Jerusalem; it was a welcome sound when I heard them saying, We will go into the Lord's house. There if our will is good, you will find room for us, so that we shall wish for nothing else but to remain in your house for ever."]

The spring to be rejoined was not the eternal one "that the nightly Ram doesn't despoil"; as if the extraordinary ascensional force that ignites Dante's words in *Paradise* were indeed lost for us; but that there would be a possible "descension" (let's dare to coin the word) towards what is most humble in this world.

∾

Strangely: here it is not even birds that serve as guides or messengers, nor those flowing waters which we understand as taking our mind along with them; but that low vegetation, which appears almost motionless and sometimes dark, with which, with a little luck, we will one day be clothed.

∿

But ultimately, what does all this mean? Once again I have not deciphered in these prairies a response that can be translated into formulas, frozen into a rule: I have experienced all this rather like . . . what? Like a gaze, or the touch of a hand, whose influence goes far beyond that of a thought and impregnates Being in a flash from head to toes. Not, if I seek to be more specific, as if it had been spoken to me: here is the image of the eternal prairies to which all the dead make their way, and among them are your family members, your poor close friends, eternally healed of hell; here is the dimmed reflection of the celestial pastures, dimmed because seeing them would burn your eyes; this would be, in a sense, too simple, too clear. No, rather, it would be as if *this* were said, or better, suggested, shown, offered to the eyes: because this enigma has remained an enigma and shines forth as such, it somehow puts into balance the other image (that of the hellish storm), it absorbs it, redeems it. I know the extent to which this can seem inane and not very convincing, but... It is not a symbol; it is at once closer to and more remote from me than a symbol, more naïve and more surreptitious, weaker and more powerful. Nor is it an explanation, an illumination. The touch of a hand, near a limit that one will not cross alive; uncrossable, indeed, but because it is uncrossable, it is incomprehensibly open. A wall so much a wall that it no longer closes off the path. A night so much a night that it gently casts light on one's footsteps.

Postface

TODAY, IN DECEMBER 2013, I must add a few comments. I first busied myself with the text in section II above, which results from some rather long trial-and-error experimentation, at the end of November 1988, at the very time when I was sending to the *Nouvelle Revue Française* the initial section whose pages, as far as they are concerned, had imposed themselves without difficulties, in the emotion of the moment, to my mind. At the beginning of the year 1990, I had sent the text that follows those initial pages, exactly as it is found here as section II, to Jean-Pierre Dauphin, who will have been, during those years, the first reader of the manuscripts that I was thinking about publishing at Gallimard, for which he was one of the most zealous servants. (I have never understood very well why he had elected me his "favorite author" among those published by that publishing company, given the extent to which our personal make-ups and tastes diverged; but this predilection moved me and was more than once precious, because Dauphin could be, in spite of this, usefully severe.) On that occasion, therefore, he notably responded: "Because I am a reader, I would much prefer, as far as you are concerned, that you pursue this further—I do not mean revise it; only that you go all the way to the end of your hesitations and take this text (this is no pun) to that *Notebook of Greenery* of which it is in fact the overture."

Coming from him, this reception clearly lacked enthusiasm; and because I did not wish, perhaps out of pure laziness, to take the text any farther, those pages remained at the back of a drawer. Only in January 2003 did a letter from José-Flore Tappy—another confidant of my writing, even before she began to devote herself, with such patient dedication, to the preparation of the Pléiade volume—remind me that I had submitted them to her in response to a request, for unpublished texts, coming from somewhere I no longer remember, and that she had chosen them for this purpose.

Ten years have thus gone by since then, during which, to say the least, my vague impulses to write have increasingly become rare, while my natural laziness has worsened . . . All the same, I would reread those pages now and then, without ever feeling any desire to revise them; but without ever resolving to destroy them, either. In addition, probably persisting in me was a great concern to remain fair towards an author whom I have never ceased admiring (yet, as is evident in section II, not without serious reservations sometimes) and towards a man for whom I have never ceased nurturing great affection.

What can I say about our long relationship, now that I have almost reached the age when he himself died?

That, undeniably, its foundations were not absolutely solid. When I was barely more than twenty years old, to the almost inevitable question raised by an elder to a "beginner"—"Who is your favorite poet?"—I responded first to Ungaretti in Rome in 1946, then to Ponge, a little later: "Rilke." If the elder of the two, Ungaretti, made a frank face while asking me if Rilke weren't "a sort of D'Annunzio," Ponge said nothing, but surely thought no less. I put myself forward in this way, moreover with great shyness, as a "lyric poet" of the worst species. (I am sure that, basically, neither man knew Rilke's oeuvre, of which they couldn't care less . . .) However, it happens that I have also been capable, or guilty, of a perhaps dangerous eclecticism in terms of admiration, in all fields of art. Reading back then, and already running the risk of commenting on very different kinds of poets, as I had done for *L'Oeillet, la guêpe, le mimosa* (The Carnation, The Wasp, The Mimosa), which was my first article in praise of Ponge in 1946, I above all let my emotion speak and, with respect to these writings, my enthusiasm. And when, soon afterwards, I had the privilege of visiting him at his apartment on the rue Lhomond, how could I not have listened to Ponge, at the time in a full period of creativity, invention and combat, not religiously but with a kind of delighted attentiveness, warmed as I was by the sunlight of his firm beliefs? (By doing so, nothing prevented me from keeping my uncertainties, in fact less uncertain than I thought, to myself, without the idea ever occurring to me to put them forward in opposition to the beaming authority that emanated from he who, in fact, did not want to be called a "poet.")

Later as well, when my own work had begun to assert itself in my first volumes published by Gallimard, Ponge himself was very careful about expressing the surely sometimes very serious reservations that those books must have inspired in him. Often, in fact, in regard to these kinds of more or less hidden contradictions, I have been tempted to invert the Latin adage "amicus Plato, sed magis amica veritas" ["Plato is my friend, but truth is a better friend"] into its contrary: "amica veritas, sed magis amicus Plato" ["Truth is my friend, but Plato is a better friend"] . . . One example among many that I can henceforth avow: what would have happened to my bonds of friendship with André du Bouchet, however close they were, if I had admitted to him one day that I did not share his unqualified adherence to Tal Coat's artistic oeuvre? Uncompromising as he was, wouldn't he have been capable of quarreling with me over a difference of opinion which, to my eyes, had little importance?

To come back to Francis Ponge, I believe—with the benefits of hindsight and while rereading our correspondence, which indeed extends from 1947 to 1986— that my inverted adage fully applied to each of us, and that I can be deeply happy about this. And of the pages that I drafted with great care for the *Cahier de l'Herne: Francis Ponge* volume little before his death, I would say that there is not one line that does not express exactly what I think, of the man and his oeuvre.

A single serious shadow will have passed one day over this undeniable friendship, therefore, and, once again, despite its fragile foundations. I discovered its gravity ten years after the death of Ponge, in his correspondence with Jean Tortel—so much more deeply closer to him. The letter is dated 15 August 1968: "But have you read the most recent issue of *L'Éphémère* (Dupin, des Forêts, du Bouchet)? It is really distressing. Of that generation, what can we still hope for?? And Jaccottet's book . . .?? The former are grotesque, the latter is disgusting." I must admit that, in this instance, one of his fits of anger and "disgust" to which he often gave full rein, in fact with a kind of jubilation—and as if he were once again throwing the great showy fits of anger of the surrealists—made me shudder for a moment; only a moment, the time it took me to say to myself how well I understood him, at least as far as I was concerned.

I have thus leafed through the book in question, *L'Entretien des Muses*, which remains to my eyes, however superficial it is, a good invitation to discover or reread nearly thirty French-language twentieth-century poets, from Claudel to Pierre Oster. Ponge is one of the rare poets in the book who received two articles, dated 1962 and 1965, and supplemented by a "Note" (1967). It is difficult to deny that the warmest and liveliest admiration appears in them; nothing to be "disgusted" about. But it is also clear that, in the concluding essay of the volume, while I was pointing to the danger, for some of the best poets of the day, of sometimes speaking a clan language and of letting themselves be enclosed in it, I must have touched a very sensitive spot in Ponge.

My father-in-law had died in 1966, in my presence, and this had been "my first death." Somewhere, in the *Lessons* that I drew from this experience, is found the line "the earth which bore us quakes." More than the visit to the insane asylum evoked in the same final pages, it is this inner seism to which I owed the reaction expressed in these pages against a certain form of language that could crop up, at the time, in literature. (In 2010, some forty years later, in my acceptance speech for the Schiller Prize, one will be able to notice that a much more general earthquake, affecting the entire world, had more seriously shaken my confidence in all poetry, even the purest.)

To come back to 1968: Francis Ponge thus had the right to sense himself targeted and, from his standpoint, very unfairly. But one can also see, in this same passage of his 15 August letter to Jean Tortel, that the most recent issue of *L'Éphémère*, at which he had so many friends, had "distressed" him. In fact, that year, it was the whole May 1968 insurrection that was exasperating him—he later spoke to me about it, more than once. Jean Tortel, who was more levelheaded by nature and who was going to publish in this same review soon thereafter, was very careful not to react to this fit of rage . . .

Moved by joy, I look again at this photo that I took—I who have never been the slightest photographer—in the entrance courtyard of Le Tertre, during the summer of 1959: it is the very image that it pleases me to retain, today, of a friendship to which many passages of Francis Ponge's letters bear witness without the slightest equivocation and which lasted until the last years of his life—how to express it?—above, or below, that is, more deeply than, our differences, which only exceptionally threatened it. I remain happy, proud, and grateful for the chance that brought us together, and perhaps still more decidedly now that these pages have at last taken on the form of a little book.

Notes

For the original French edition of this book, Philippe Jaccottet drafted five endnotes. I have incorporated them into my own endnotes and added several more. Unless otherwise specified, all translations of quotations are mine. Francis Ponge's collected writings are available in two Gallimard-Pléiade volumes (*Oeuvres complètes*, I, 1999; II, 2002): in the references, "I" and "II" designate the respective volumes, followed by the page numbers.

(p. 9) In French: "Beaux et grands bastimens d'éternelle structure" . . . "Beau parc et beaux jardins, qui dans vostre closture / Avez tousjours des fleurs et des ombrages vers" . . . These lines by François de Malherbe (1555–1628) are discussed in Ponge's *Pour un Malherbe* (Éditions Gallimard, 1965 / revised edition 1977), a book now included in the second volume of the Pléiade edition (2002) of Ponge's works. The French title emphasizes an "approach" to Malherbe and his oeuvre, as if

Ponge were founding his "essay" on the etymological sense of the term; and, arguably, the title also puns with the word "herbier" ("herbarium" and notably a set of illustrations of plants). On pages 1454–1458 of the second volume of the Pléiade edition, a table lists the references to the quotations of Malherbe's poetry that Ponge uses in his book. The references to lines by Malherbe that are cited by Jaccottet can be found there. Malherbe was an essential model for Ponge. In *Pour un Malherbe*, he writes: "I like everything in Malherbe, to whom only Baudelaire sometimes comes close, and La Fontaine, in their best moments."

(p. 10) The "Carousel of the Four Elements" ("Carousel des Quatre Éléments") also alludes to a poem by Malherbe.

(p. 10) Ponge wrote his poetic prose text "L'Asparagus" for a livre d'artiste (published in 1963) with the French painter Jean Fautrier (1898–1964). II, 324–327.

(p. 10) For the interview with André Breton and Pierre Reverdy, see I, 684. When Ponge refers to "as low as possible" (in French he uses the popular expression "le 36ᵉ dessous"), he specifies: "Poverty" is "the only locus, I would not say of the empire of [poetic] speech, but of its energetic exercise as low as possible. Moreover, because it is by taking off from below that one has some chance of rising. Finally, because it is with lead that one makes gold, not with silver or platinum."

(p. 11) The lines by Charles Baudelaire ("envoyant son coeur et sa pensée à une Électre lointaine qui essuyait naguère son front baigné de sueur" . . .) are taken from the dedication, "To J.G.F.," of *Les Paradis artificiels* (*The Artificial Paradises*, 1860).

(p. 11) Jaccottet refers to the character Elvire in Molière's play *Dom Juan ou le Festin de pierre* (1665 / 1682). Ponge discusses Don Juan with respect to Albert Camus's *The Myth of Sisyphus* in "Réflexions en lisant *L'essai sur l'absurde*," I, 206. In his *Papiers collés* (volume I, Gallimard, 1960, pp. 190–193), Georges Perros writes insightfully of Ponge's method: "Telling a story, a narration, is not at stake, but a conquest. [Ponge] is the Don Juan of things." A selection of Perros's incisive aphorisms and short prose is available in English in *Paper Collage* (translated by John Taylor, Seagull Books, 2015).

(p. 12) "The Lord is my shepherd . . ." Psalm 23.

(p. 12) Christian Rist (b. 1952), French actor and stage director. For the lines from Ponge's "Le Pré", see II, 343: "Transportés tout à coup par une sorte d'enthousiasme paisible, / En faveur d'une vérité, aujourd'hui, qui soit verte."

(p. 13) For Ponge's interview with Loïs Dahlin, see II, 1433. For the full interview: "Entretien avec Francis Ponge," *The French Review*, vol. LIII, No. 2, December 1980, pp. 271–272; *Cahiers de l'Herne*, No. 51, 1986, pp. 521–531.

(p. 13) Shepherds indeed play an important role for the Spanish poet Luis de Góngora y Argote (1561–1627), two selections of whose poetry Jaccottet has translated: *Les Solitudes* (La Dogana, 1983) and *Treize sonnets et un fragment* (La Dogana, 1985).

(p. 14) Rilke's lines are taken from his "Spanish Trilogy", which the German poet wrote between December 1912 and January 1913, in Ronda, Spain, during an existential crisis. In German: "Abwechselnd weilt er und zieht, wie selber der Tag, / und Schatten der Wolken / durchgehn ihn, als dächte der Raum / langsam Gedanken für ihn."

(p. 15) Malherbe's original French lines: "Apollon à portes ouvertes / Laisse indifféremment cueillir / Les belles feuilles tousjours vertes / Qui gardent les noms de vieillir."

(p. 16) Chambon-sur-Lignon is a protestant village in the Cévennes, famous because of the number of Jews who were hidden and saved there by the villagers, beginning in 1940, during the Second World War. Ponge first visited it in 1924 and returned frequently thereafter. One of his best-known books, *Le Parti pris des choses* (*Partisan of Things*, 1942), was written during his vacations in Chambon-sur-Lignon. His book *La Fabrique du pré* (1971) refers directly to a meadow near Chambon-sur-Lignon.

(**p. 16**) Rilke's lines are from the beginning of the "Ninth Duino Elegy": ". . . als Lorbeer, ein wenig dunkler als alles / andere Grün, mit kleinen Wellen an jedem / Blattrand (wie eines Windes Lächeln) . . ."

(**p. 17**) For Ponge's text on the death of the artist Georges Braque (1882–1963), see "Braque ou un méditatif à l'oeuvre," II, 696–721.

(**p. 18**) Malherbe's original French lines: "L'an n'aura plus d'hyver, le jour n'aura plus d'ombre, / Et les perles sans nombre / Germeront dans la Seine au milieu des graviers."

(**p. 24**) Ponge refers to Hamlet early on in his oeuvre, notably at the beginning of *Douze petits écrits* (Twelve Little Writings, 1926) and in a somewhat satirical mode.

(p. 24) Malherbe's original French lines: "Les muses, les neuf belles fées."

(p. 24) "À propos du grand recueil," "Malherbe comme modèle," and "Note" make up the Francis Ponge chapter of *L'Entretien des Muses* (Gallimard, 1968, pp. 115–128), which is one of Jaccottet's collections of essays. In his "Note," Jaccottet writes these words, which he paraphrases further on in the present volume about Ponge: "In one or two places appears, more or less palpably, a danger which, it seems to me, threatens several of the best writers today: that of letting themselves be enclosed in a world of references (which will be, for example, and according to the case, Paulhan, or Barthes, or Heidegger), a world in which, despite all the force of his personality, [Ponge] tends to adopt a clan language—a clan that is, and such is the case here, an undeniable elite—the language of his critics, his interpreters."

(p. 25) For the English title of Ponge's book, *Le Parti pris des choses* (1942), I borrow the title of Joshua Corey and Jean-Luc Garneau's translation, *Partisan of Things* (Kenning Editions, 2016).

(p. 25) For the English title of Ponge's book, *Le Soleil placé en* *abîme* (1954 / 1961), I borrow the title of Serge Gavronsky's translation, *The Sun Placed in the Abyss* (Sun, 1977).

(p. 26) Ponge writes about Fautrier in "Fautrier, d'un seul bloc fougueusement équarri," II, 608–611, especially p. 611. See also "Fautrier, Body and Soul," II, 744–746.

(p. 30) *Les Indes galantes* (*The Gallant Indies*) by Jean-Philippe Rameau (1683–1764) is an opera first staged in 1735.

(p. 31) For "La Société du génie," I, 635.

(p. 31) In this passage about Jean-Philippe Rameau, it is important to know that Philippe Jaccottet is a fine amateur harpsichordist. References to Baroque music, and other periods of music, appear regularly in his writings. Jaccottet's title *L'Entretien des Muses* comes from Jean-Philippe Rameau's famous harpsichord piece, which is included in the "Suite in D Major" (*Pièces de Clavessin*, 1724).

(p. 35) For "Le Carnet du bois de pins," see I, 377. Jaccottet's *Paysages avec figures absentes* has been translated by Mark Treharne into English as *Landscapes with Absent Figures* (Birmingham, United Kingdom: Delos Press / London:

Menard Press, 1997). In the original French book, the text mentioned here is titled "Travaux au lieu-dit l'Étang," which Treharne renders as "Working at L'Étang." The quotations are in my translation.

(p. 37) In his important essay "Remarques," which concludes *L'Entretien des Muses*, Jaccottet outlines his view of the French poetry of the day, evoking the poetics of Ponge, Paul Claudel, Saint-John Perse, René Char, Guillevic, Jean Follain, Jean Tortel, Jean Tardieu, Yves Bonnefoy, Michel Deguy, Jean Grosjean, Jacques Dupin, André du Bouchet, Henri Thomas, Pierre Jean Jouve, André Breton, Jules Supervielle, and Henri Michaux. Among the passages pertinent to Jaccottet's critique of Ponge, these words (pp. 305–6): "As in every art of high civilization, the equilibrium of all the human qualities, which is indispensable if the work of art is to be fully accomplished, runs the risk in every moment of being broken, and to be broken especially because of an excessive mastery inducing virtuosity, ornamentation, the overabundance or the extreme intricacy of rhetorical figures. Moreover, in whatever direction the disequilibrium lies, one will note that each quality, if it develops alone at the expense of the others (for example, attentiveness to the world, so characteristic of the majority of contemporary poets, perhaps out of a fear of losing one's footing, or, on the contrary, pure reflection or attentiveness to words), becomes too visible, a kind of *screen*; and the poem, whose role had been that of opening towards the center, now blocks the reader's gaze or deviates it from that center. The reader then thinks (at best): What a sharp eye! What precise prosody! What deep thinking! All of which are reflections that do not come to mind when reading an *accomplished* poem or a fragment thereof; and such a poem is so rare because the equilibrium, of the intellectual, moral, and sensitive qualities that it requires, can only be exceptional. On the other hand, the exclusion from every community, which is the lot of the modern poet if he does not commit himself to a cause, a commitment in which one notices his poetry necessarily deteriorating, indeed seems to lead to, little by little, the unconscious creation of closed systems (the poet surrounded by various satellites: disciples, critics, a few readers); even if the poet is by no means responsible for this, at the heart of such systems can form an equally closed language in which the temptations of mastery can only be aggravated: intricacy, obscurity, and, worse than these, a tone of haughty *certitude* (going sometimes all the way to self-complacency) which stiffens all the more as the system in which it is elaborated is increasingly better closed."

(p. 39) Jean Paulhan (1884–1968) was a writer and an important editor at Gallimard. He remains well-known in modern French literature for having discovered, and been the first reader of, many key writers.

(p. 40) In his own Notes to this book, in regard to "the invasion of writing by a certain philosophical language," Jaccottet signals out a passage from Schelling's *Clara: Über den Zusammenhang der Natur mit der Geisterwelt*, by using a French translation (found in *Clara, ou Du lien de la nature au monde des esprits*, translated by Elisabeth Kessler, Éditions de L'Herne, 1984, p. 133). Here is the same passage in Fiona Steinkamp's English version: "Why do today's philosophers find it so impossible to write at least a little in the same way that they speak? Are these terrible artificial words absolutely necessary, can't the same thing be said in a more natural way, and does a book have to be quite unenjoyable to be philosophical? I don't mean the obscurity that comes from depth and that only those can see whose eyes are accustomed to looking away from the surface. The deepest, I feel, must also be the clearest; just as what is clearest, e.g., a crystal, by virtue of being such, doesn't seem to get closer to me, but instead seems to withdraw and to become more obscure, and just as I can look into a drop of water as if into an abyss. At any rate, depth must be distinguished from opacity." (*Clara or,*

On Nature's Connection to the Spirit World, translated with an introduction by Fiona Steinkamp, SUNY Press, 2002.)

(p. 40) *Leçons*, which has been translated into English by Mark Treharne in the bilingual edition *Leçons / Learning* (Birmingham, United Kingdom: Delos Press, 2001). "The earth which bore us quakes" is Treharne's translation for "La terre qui portait tremble." In this long poetic sequence, Jaccottet evokes the death of his father-in-law, Louis Haesler. Jaccottet also evokes this death in *Patches of Sunlight, or of Shadow* (translated by John Taylor, Seagull Books, 2020).

(p. 41) In his own Notes, Jaccottet writes: For Bernard Böschenstein, who has devoted a pertinent study to this hymn, "what springs out purely" designates fire. The poet's function, in this time of waiting, is to veil so that it will not consume us. But the river itself seems to me to be a "pure springing out" from the source, from the foundation, from the origin; the river is also this "innocent water" asked for, as sustenance, at the beginning of another hymn, "Patmos."

(p. 41) Rimbaud's line, "l'étincelle d'or de la lumière *nature*," is found in "Faim" ("Hunger") in the *Une saison en enfer* (*A Season in Hell*). In translations, this line has been rendered as, for example, "a spark of gold of *natural* light" and "a spark of gold of *pure* light." But Rimbaud indeed writes "nature," not "naturelle" or "pure," and the word is italicized.

(p. 43) One of Pascal's best-known "pensées" or "thoughts" is this: "When we see a natural style, we are astonished and delighted, for we expected to see an author and we find a man, whereas those who have good tastes and who, in seeing a book and thinking that they find a man, are astonished to find an author. *Plus poetice quam humane locutus es.* [You have spoken more like a poet than a human being.] Those honor nature well who teach it to speak of everything, even theology."

(p. 44) Ponge's *Cinq Sapates* was published by Georges Braque in 1950, in a hundred copies, each with five engravings by the artist. A "sapate" is a considerable gift, hidden in something ordinary, which is given to a friend. See "La Terre" (I, 749), "Les Olives" (I, 753), "La Cruche" (I, 751), "Ébauche d'un poisson" (I, 754), "Le Volet, suivi de sa scholie" (I, 757).

(p. 44) For "My Creative Method," see I, 515, 821.

(p. 47) Jaccottet mentions in his own Notes that he quotes the poem, in French, from Buson's *Haïku*, translated from the Japanese by Nobuko Imamura and Alain Gouvret, Paris, Éditions Arfuyen, 1988.

(p. 49) The translation of the first two lines of Goethe's poem is by Henry Wadsworth Longfellow. I have modernized the spelling of "o'er":

> Über allen Gipfeln
> Ist Ruh' . . .

> O'er all the heights
> is quiet . . .

(p. 50) In his own Notes, Jaccottet writes apropos of "Wanderers Nachtlied" ["The Wanderer's Night Song"]: I have written elsewhere [that] this little poem offers an example, which is remarkable to my mind, of the extreme difficulty of translating a literary work that is perfect to this extent, to which the subtlety of the structure takes nothing away from the entirely natural appearance of confidence. (Perhaps this combination is specific to Goethe's genius, which would explain that no French translation, at least to my knowledge, has never given justice to this poem.) Without its rhymes, its inner assonances, not much remains of the poem; but let us suppose a translator capable, by means of an extreme virtuosity, of working out equivalents; how could he, at the same time, preserve the natural appearance as well, the pure simplicity of this murmur? This is why I prefer to give here only a prose translation:

> Au-dessus des montagnes règne à présent une par-
> faite paix.
> C'est à peine si, dans les cimes des arbres, tu perçois
>   un souffle encore.
> Dans la forêt, les oiseaux se sont tus.
> Patience ! Bientôt, la paix te sera donnée à toi aussi.

To this version I add a legitimate sigh: "What a wretched shame! It is as if one explained a gaze, a snowflake."

P. S. (and belated regret): in 1993, the appearance of a few translations by Jean Tardieu, which he gathered around the theme of *L'Élégie de Marienbad* and which is the title of the small volume, has contradicted me, at least a little. Here is his version, not entirely convincing all the same:

> Sur toutes les cimes
> La paix.
> Au faîte des arbres
> Tu saisiras

Un souffle à peine.
Au bois se taisent les oiseaux.
Attends ! Bientôt
Toi-même aussi
Reposeras.

(p. 52) The poetic prose text "Blazon in Green and White" can be found bilingually in *And, Nonetheless: Selected Prose and Poetry 1990–2009*, translated by John Taylor, Chelsea Editions, 2011, pp. 40–57. Otherwise, in the Pléiade edition of Jaccottet's collected writings, pp. 752–759.

(p. 53) *The Triumph of Flora* (1627–1628) is a painting by Nicolas Poussin (1594–1665).

(p. 54) In the original French edition of this book, Jaccottet quotes from Yves Bonnefoy's translation of Shakespeare's *The Winter's Tale* (IV, iv, 127–135):

Oh, que ceux-là
Me manquent, pour vous en faire des guirlandes,
Et, mon très doux ami,
Pour l'en joncher sur tout, sur tout le corps.
— Eh, comme un mort ?
— Non, comme un pré, pour les jeux de l'amour

Et son repos. Un mort ? Oui, pour l'ensevelir
Bien vivant toujours dans mes bras. Allons, prenez
    vos fleurs.
Je crois bien que je joue comme j'ai vu faire
Aux pastorales de Pentecôte ... Sûr que c'est cette
    robe
Qui a changé mon esprit

Bonnefoy's translation, as Jaccottet himself specifies, was first published by the Club Français du Livre (Paris, 1957), with a new edition at Mercure de France in 1994. Note that Bonnefoy translates Shakespeare's "bank" in the line "No, like a bank for love to lie and play on" as "pré" (meadow, prairie). Basing his observations on Bonnefoy's translation and associating them with his other remarks about "meadows" in this book, Jaccottet subsequently uses the words "pré" and "prairie," whereas I use "grassy bank" and then "grassy embankment" to evoke meadows and prairies but also to remain close to Shakespeare's text.

(p. 56) Jaccottet refers to Dante's *Paradise*, Canto I, 91–93 "Tu non se' in terra, si come tu credi; / ma folgore, fuggendo il proprio sito, / non corse come tu che ad esso riedi." I interpret "sito" here as "home."

(p. 56) Saint Augustine's text is from *Confessions* (Book 13, chapter 9). In the original French edition, Jaccottet quotes the passage directly in Latin, with a French translation only in his Notes. The English translation that I have inserted into the text is from *Confessions*, translated by R. S. Pine-Coffin, Penguin Books, 1961.

(p. 58) Dante, *Paradise,* Canto 28, 117: "che notturno Ariete non dispoglia."

(p. 64) *Cahier de verdure* has been entirely translated as *Notebook of Greenery* in *And, Nonetheless: Selected Prose and Poetry 1990–2009*, translated by John Taylor, Chelsea Editions, 2011.

(p. 64) José-Flore Tappy (b. 1954) is a Swiss poet, whose poetry is entirely available in my translation: *Sheds / Hangars: Collected Poems 1983–2013* (The Bitter Oleander Press, 2014); and *Trás-os-Montes* (The MadHat Press, 2020). She was the general editor of the Gallimard-Pléiade volume of Jaccottet's collected writings: *Oeuvres*, Gallimard, 2014.

(p. 66) "L'Oeillet" (I, 356, 435), "La Guêpe" (I, 339, 434), "Le Mimosa" (I, 366, 436). These three texts were published together by Mermod in 1946.

(p. 67) Tal Coat was a French painter (1905–1985) who was the friend of many poets and often collaborated with them on *livres d'artiste* and other projects. For Jaccottet's friendship with André du Bouchet, see his *Truinas, 21 April 2001*, translated by John Taylor, the Fortnightly Review Press, 2018.

(p. 67) The special volume on Ponge to which Jaccottet refers is *Le Cahier de l'Herne: Francis Ponge*, No. 51, edited by Jean-Marie Gleize, Éditions de l'Herne, 1986. It was partly reprinted and published by Le Livre de Poche in 1989.

(p. 68) The path-breaking literary review *L'Éphémère* was founded by Yves Bonnefoy, André du Bouchet, Jacques Dupin, Louis-René des Forêts, and the critic Gaëtan Picon; after the departure of Picon, in 1968, Paul Celan and the critic Michel Leiris joined the editorial committee. Twenty issues appeared during the years 1966–1972.

(p. 68) Jean Tortel (1904–1993) was a French poet. Jaccottet evokes his relationship with Tortel in *Patches of Sunlight, or of Shadow* (translated by John Taylor, Seagull Books, 2020).

(p. 68) In *L'Entretien des Muses*, its concluding essay, "Remarques," and also the "Note" on Ponge, evokes a "clan language."

(p. 69) Jaccottet's acceptance speech, "Le Combat inégal" ("The Unequal Battle") for the Schiller Prize is comprised in the Pléiade volume of Jaccottet's collected writings, pp. 1342–1346. He notably raises the issue of the role of poetry with respect to the horrors of the outside world. "More and more often," he writes, "I would think of that *lied* of Mahler's *Kindertotenlieder* in which the father, who knows that his children are dead, sighs: 'In diesem Wetter, in diesem Braus, / Nie hätt' ich gelassen die Kinder hinaus' ['In such terrible weather, I should never have let the children go outside']. But Mahler was still able to draw admirable music from this drama, whereas today's storm threatens the very possibility of any music. My poem from 1977 came back to mind. Promising myself to no longer despair of any outcome, I raised in this poem, in conclusion, a question full of anxiety: 'mais il y a presque trop / de poids du côté sombre où je nous vois descendre / et redresser avec de l'invisible chaque jour, / qui le pourrait encore, qui l'a pu?' ['but there is almost too much / weight on the dark side into which I see us descend / and who could still, who has been able to, / raise every day back up with the invisible?']." The latter lines are found in "Autres chants," p. 547.

(p. 70) The Château du Tertre was the French novelist Roger Martin du Gard's residence during the years 1925–1958 and now houses his museum. Jaccottet was Martin du Gard's literary executor, a story that he tells in *Patches of Sunlight, or of Shadow* (translated by John Taylor, Seagull Books, 2020).

From left to right: Odette Ponge, Anne-Marie Jaccottet, and Francis Ponge at Christiane Martin du Gard's château "Le Tertre," in 1959.

About the author

Born in Switzerland and a longtime resident of France, PHILIPPE JACCOTTET (b. 1925) is one of the essential European poets. He has been awarded numerous European literary prizes, including the Petrarch Prize, the Goncourt Prize for Poetry, the Friedrich-Hölderlin Prize, the Schiller Prize, the Cino-Del-Duca Prize, and the Grand Prix Suisse de littérature. In 2014, his collected writings were issued as a volume in Gallimard's prestigious "Pléiade" series, a rare honor for a living author. His most recent collections of poems and poetic prose texts are available in John Taylor's translation: *And, Nonetheless: Selected Prose and Poetry 1990–2009* (Chelsea Editions). Taylor has also translated Jaccottet's *The Pilgrim's Bowl: Giorgio Morandi* (Seagull Books, 2015), *A Calm Fire and other Travel Writings* (Seagull Books, 2019), *Patches of Sunlight, or of Shadow* (Seagull Books, 2020), and *Truinas, 21 April 2001* (The Fortnightly Review Press, 2018), which evokes the funeral of his friend André du Bouchet. Other books by Jaccottet have been translated by Tess Lewis for Seagull Books: *Obscurity*, his only novel, and two volumes of his *Seedtime* notebook series.

About the translator

JOHN TAYLOR was born in Des Moines in 1952. He has lived in France since 1977. Among his many translations of French, Italian, and Modern Greek literature are books by Jacques Dupin, José-Flore Tappy, Pierre Voélin, Pierre Chappuis, Pierre-Albert Jourdan, Catherine Colomb, Lorenzo Calogero, Alfredo de Palchi, Franca Mancinelli, Elias Petropoulos, and Elias Papadimitrakopoulos. He is the author of several volumes of short prose and poetry, most recently *The Dark Brightness* (Xenos Books, 2017), *Grassy Stairways* (The MadHat Press, 2017), *Remembrance of Water & Twenty-Five Trees* (The Bitter Oleander Press, 2018) and a "double book" coauthored with the Swiss poet Pierre Chappuis, *A Notebook of Clouds & A Notebook of Ridges* (The Fortnightly Review Press, 2019).

Black Square Editions was started in 1999 with the intention of publishing translations of little-known books by well-known poets and fiction writers, as well as the work of emerging and established authors. After twenty years, we are still proceeding book by book.

Black Square Editions—a subsidiary of Off the Park Press, Inc, a tax-exempt (501c3) nonprofit organization—would like to thank the following for their support.

Tim Barry
Robert Bunker
Catherine Kehoe
Taylor Moore
Goldman Sachs
Pittsburgh Foundation Grant
Miles McEnery Gallery (New York, New York)
I.M. of Emily Mason & Wolf Kahn
Galerie Lelong & Co. (Paris, France)
Bernard Jacobson Gallery (London, England)
Saturnalia Books
& Anonymous Donors